3|11

If You're Happy and You Know It

Distributed by The Child's World®
1980 Lookout Drive • Mankato, MN 56003-1705
800-599-READ • www.childsworld.com

Acknowledgments
The Child's World®: Mary Berendes, Publishing Director
The Design Lab: Kathleen Petelinsek, Design and Page Production

Library of Congress Cataloging-in-Publication Data
Freeman-Hines, Laura.
  If you're happy and you know it / illustrated by Laura Freeman.
      p. cm.
  Summary: Presents the popular song that encourages everyone to express
their happiness through voice and movement. End notes list the benefits of
activity songs.
  ISBN 978-1-60253-531-2 (library bound : alk. paper)
  1. Children's songs, English—Texts. [1. Songs. 2. Happiness—Songs and
music. 3. Singing games. 4. Games.] I. Title. II. Title: If you are happy and
you know it.
  PZ8.3.F9067If 2010
  782.42–dc22 [E]   2010015201

Printed in the United States of America in Mankato, Minnesota.
July 2010
F11538

ILLUSTRATED BY LAURA FREEMAN

If you're happy
and you know it,
clap your hands.

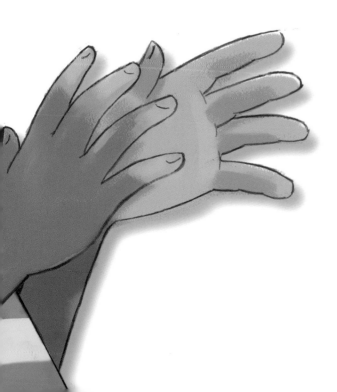

If you're happy
and you know it,
clap your hands.

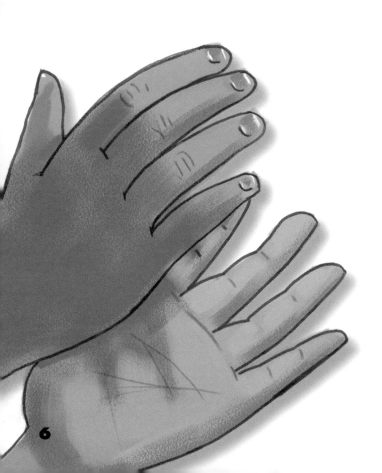

If you're happy
and you know it . . .

. . . then your face
will surely show it.

If you're happy
and you know it,

clap your hands.

SONG ACTIVITY

If you're happy and you know it, <u>clap your hands</u>.
(Clap hands twice)

If you're happy and you know it, <u>clap your hands</u>.
(Clap hands twice)

If you're happy and you know it...
Then your face will surely show it.
If you're happy and you know it, <u>clap your hands</u>.
(Clap hands twice)

Repeat the song three more times. The first time, replace the words "clap your hands" with "tap your toes." The second time, replace the words "tap your toes" with "nod your head." The last time, go back to singing the words "clap your hands" in the right spot.

BENEFITS OF CHILDREN'S POEMS AND SONGS

Children's poems and songs are more than just a fun way to pass the time. They are a rich source of intellectual, emotional, and physical development for a young child. Here are some of their benefits:

❀ Learning the words and activities builds the child's self-confidence—"I can do it all by myself!"

❀ The repetitious movements build coordination and motor skills.

❀ The close physical interaction between adult and child reinforces both physical and emotional bonding.

❀ In a context of "fun," the child learns the art of listening in order to learn.

❀ Learning the words expands the child's vocabulary. He or she learns the names of objects and actions that are both familiar and new.

❀ Repeating the words helps develop the child's memory.

❀ Learning the words is an important step toward learning to read.

❀ Reciting the words gives the child a grasp of English grammar and how it works. This enhances the development of language skills.

❀ The rhythms and rhyming patterns sharpen listening skills and teach the child how poetry works. Eventually the child learns to put together his or her own simple rhyming words— "I made a poem!"

ABOUT THE ILLUSTRATOR

Laura Freeman has been drawing pictures for as long as she can remember, and illustrating books since 1998. She's from New York City, but currently lives in Atlanta with her husband, their two children, and a very small hamster.